Through intensely personal experiences, *Optics* shows vision as a trick of light. What we see through a glass barrier we've placed between ourselves and our world is often filtered by the warps and swirls caught in that glass. We stand behind a window that is growing dark in early winter, not even noticing the creeping darkness across the glass blocking our vision. The poems explore the world reflected back by a simple piece of glass.

Also by Bob Stallworthy:

From a Call Box
Under the Sky Speaking

Optics
Bob Stallworthy

Frontenac House
Calgary, Alberta

Book design by EPIX Design Inc.
Cover photography by Neil Petrunia
Author photo: Thomas Legg

Quote on p. 55 is from page 128 of *In the City of Our Fathers* by Don Kerr Coteau Books 1992

National Library of Canada Cataloguing in Publication

Stallworthy, Bob
       Optics / Bob Stallworthy.

Poems.
ISBN 0-9732380-6-2

     I. Title.
PS8587.T2713O68 2004   C811'.54   C2004-900355-0

We acknowledge the support of the Canada Council for the Arts which last year invested $21.7 million in writing and publishing throughout Canada. We also acknowledge the support of The Alberta Foundation for the Arts.

Printed and bound in Canada.
Published by Frontenac House Ltd.
1138 Frontenac Avenue S.W.
Calgary, Alberta, T2T 1B6, Canada
Tel: 403-245-2491   Fax: 403-245-2380
editor@frontenachouse.com   www.frontenachouse.com

1 2 3 4 5 6 7 8 9   08 07 06 05 04

To my father, Dr. W. B. Stallworthy, who showed me
there was more than one way to look at the world

Acknowledgements

Some of these poems have appeared in *FreeFall, Crossing Place Anthology, Prairie Journal of Canadian Literature, Green's Magazine,* and *Under The Sky Speaking,* Snowapple Press, 1998.

A special thank you to my wife, Marilyn, who continues to believe in what I do.

Thank you to Richard Harrison for the editorial work on this manuscript as Writer in Residence at Alexandra Writers Centre and beyond.

Thank you to the Thursday night poetry group for their friendship and suggestions.

Thank you to Jan Boydol, Sharon Drummond, Cecelia Frey, Richard Stevenson, Ken Rivard, Robert Hilles and the Kensington Writers Group for their friendship.

Contents

Politics   11
Graduation   12
Moving Day   13
Just Looking   14
Window Shopping   15
Flawed Glass   16
Storm Windows   17
Window Washers   18
Broken Pane   19
Spell Broken   20
Passing By   21
Clip-Ons   22
Christmas Eyes   24
Christmas Star   25
Night Flight Reflections   26
Outside Looking In   27
The Definition of Difference   28
Mother Sometimes is Anger   29
Alpha and Omega   30
Intersection   31
Photo Album   32
Out a Window   33
Colours of a Wake   35
Down Sizing   36
Building Security   37
First Thunderstorm   38
Peeping Tom   39
Window Blind   40
Ninety Degrees to the Sun   41
Shards of Sunday   42
Remembering for Two   43
The Windows   44
No Way Out   45
Tourist   46
Pictures   47
Shelf Life   48
This Abandoned Place   49
Kept on File   50

Rear View Mirror   51
Reading About Life   52
After Lunch in the Seniors' Home   53
They   54
Not Voyeurism   56
After Thoughts on September 11   57
Street Reflections   58
Write from Your Roots   59
Mathematics   60
Before the Window Falls   62
Christmas is Coming   63
The Day my Mother Died   64
Something this Way Comes   65
Dancers of Night   66
Bubble   67
Cut and Run   68
Learning to See African   69
Surviving the Odds   70
Optics   71
Memory of Anger   72
Caught Cleaning Windows   73
Phobia   74
Cancer Flowers   75

Optics

Politics

there is no squabbling over where we sit
we are adults on a Saturday drive

words roll like tires on asphalt
ideas like prairie quarter sections fit
one against the next
our path clearly defined by the centre line

on the way home we sit in the same order
drop opinions into the spaces between the seats
wait to see which words might explode
our positions much more structured
each of us looks out our own window

Graduation

we are waiting
for our lives to begin

you've turned your back to me
your brown eyes
search through glass and mist
that dissolves and reforms
the world outside

from the other side of the living room
filling up with late afternoon
you let thoughts slip over the windowsill
away from me

unable to follow
I hear you not talking

Moving Day

you live on the twenty-sixth floor
sliding balcony doors frame
thunderstorms   sunrises   Fata Morgana

there are six years of looking out
to be cleaned off each window

on opposite sides of the balcony glass
we face our movements
exaggerated copies of each other

we are careful to point out
the places we have missed
smears left when we took the last swipe

check our handiwork
you on the other side of now
move in and out of my reflection

Just Looking

after you find the hotel
sit on the bed
check out the view

you stroll down the main street
see-thru sides on boxes
are placed side by side

   one is full of dishes
   table set as if the window decorator knew
   the next full of manikins wearing lingerie
   prices not seen anywhere

the guide book says
a side street
takes you to another attraction
   in the windows
   real live girls look back
   and
   eye contact is mandatory
   and
   it sure isn't lingerie they're selling
   and
   the prices aren't shown anywhere

you hurry back to your hotel
perhaps tomorrow
you will go shopping
if there's time you might even buy

Window Shopping

back in town after ten years
now he has to stay in the hotel

after dinner he stands
in front of the first house remembered
it isn't as big

he walks downtown stepping carefully
over sidewalk cracks
scarches the faces of the houses
for any sign of recognition

at the centre of town
he window shops for souvenirs
the windows hold nothing he wants

behind lace curtains
watchers suspicious
as he backtracks to now

Flawed Glass

       white boats on blue water
        a bit of black road disappearing into the corner
pictured on a card
all framed behind a thin blue line

that road is the way back home
black spruce   lupine-purpled ditches
a window warped like old-time glass

pain catches him unawares
mirages and words say "come back home"
he stares in the flawed window

there is one more empty space
that will not be filled this summer

Storm Windows

the father Fall ritual
storm windows on the house

they never fit tightly
let winter storms whistle their way into the house
cold wind on floors
clears rooms of cornered words

each Spring
the windows stored at the back
in the dusty garage
forgotten disconnected arguments
stacked against each other
cracks waiting to be Summer-painted over

we thought we left them behind
when the storms broke over the new house
those windows rattled
just like the ones in the old house
cold swept the corners clean
scattered us

in my own house
every Fall I repeat my father's ritual
take the screens off
put the storm windows on
the same father hope in my fingers

Window Washers

tiny lives cradled forty floors up
suspended from sky hooks

piece by piece they work their way
across the patchwork sky
white   blue   burnt orange   gold
laid out in squares of glass
as far as their eyes can see

they wash off birdshit   dust left over
from two weeks' worth of traffic jammed
bits of words discarded into the air
by pedestrians passing beneath them

on the ground
the shirts and ties   the high heels and pantyhose
pretend not to notice these skywashers

the window washers reach their horizon
the sun drops out of sight
turns the day to black
office lights are stars

Broken Pane

stacking fire wood
I still remember the crash   wood through glass
now I don't stack wood
along any window wall

this afternoon we sit in your apartment
three thousand miles from that house
stare out your living room window
remark on the Fall colours
the way a neighbour nine floors down
stacked wood   a wooden Pisa
too close to a window

I want to tell you
I have the putty   the glazing points   the glass
I know now how to fix that window
I want to
but you don't remember
it was ever broken

Spell Broken

remember Herman's Hermits
"Two Silhouettes on the Shade"

as a boy
in the lightning strikes of teenage love
I played the grooves off that record
until my parents threatened to spin
platter and player
in a sidewalk-bound trajectory
out my bedroom window

I hear my high untrained voice
sing along
imagine myself crashing
slivers of vinyl love and electrical components
smouldering in front of my girl's house
(what was her name now?)
watching two shadows on the pull-down blind

always knew what I would do
wouldn't make the mistake in the first place
I knew where my girlfriend lived
wouldn't bang on her door
no matter how mad I was
would walk away
wouldn't look back

Passing By

after ten o'clock
there are windows still lit
behind one the white light of a reading lamp
a favourite from an almost-forgotten home
the one next door the blue
of an institutional night light

in the first room
a man sits in his own La-Z-Boy
his white hair combed to cover the bald spot
reads   the book rests in his lap
an arthritic finger keeping his place
waits for the night nurse to bring sleep

inside the blue room
a woman too small for the bed
her face the repository for wrinkles
keeps nightmares where they should be
between wall and ceiling

tonight there is somebody
standing at a window of a stairwell landing
eye to eye with darkness
unsure of where she is going
hoping she's found Jacob's Ladder

Clip-Ons

he doesn't remember a time
before she wore glasses
there are only pictures in black and white
a woman younger than he is now

in the back yard
under the apple tree big enough for climbing
handbag over one arm
she poses in a summer dress
the hem reaching to the middle of her knee

at the Dominion Day parade
someone must have taken her picture watching him
ride his bike with a cardboard horse's head
on the handlebars
paper streams woven into the spokes
he wears a cowboy hat and double holsters

her sunglasses are clip-ons
bought in the Rexall Drugstore
where he sat on red and silver metal toadstools
at the ice cream counter
feet dangling

tried on glasses from the wire rack by the door
that spun his summer face with a tag for a nose
and made his eyes blue   rose   yellow

now he doesn't go to the parade
the drugstore in the shopping mall isn't Rexall
there isn't an ice cream counter
no metal toadstool seats
the wire rack isn't by the door

he wears clip-on sunglasses
looks for a world
that should have her in it

Christmas Eyes

at the party
in front of the artificial tree
your eyes wide open
mouth in that O
arms embrace it all

on the lowest bough
you find a silver globe
large enough to hold
your whole face in its shine
point to the baby in the ball

for an instant
we hold the ball together
suspended in glass

someday I hope you can reach out
touch it
without breaking it

Christmas Star

Christmas Eve
the stars are lights
hung on boughs of sky

in Sackville then
we looked out a kitchen window
half covered with frost

I'm not sure I really believed
but it crossed my mind
to check just in case
to look for a small red light
high in the sky

we picked out the brightest star
wondered if it was The Star
I doubt that either of us really believed

tonight one star burns
brighter than all the rest
perhaps it is the same star
perhaps mother and son
watch it from opposite sides
its light the bridge

but that would require belief

Night Flight Reflections

35,000 feet deep in the night sky
we are a shooting star

red   green   white flashes
travel earth bound

we reach trajectory's end
descend into a Milky Way of streets

among the sleepless lights
someone at a window
watches us fall from the stars

Outside Looking In

sometimes looking at you father
it is looking in from the outside
watching a stranger
fill his day with forgetting

this man has trouble getting out of his chair
has to regain his balance as he stands
before he strikes out into the world
kitchen   hallway   bedroom   bathroom

sometimes this man looks at me
eyes clouded with too many questions
trying to decide whether he knows the person he sees

sometimes when I look at you father
it is standing outside a one-way window
looking in at me
thirty-five years older

sometimes when we look at each other
we are looking in the same direction

The Definition of Difference

he wears his belligerence
like ancient chain mail

      we glare at each other
      through an unbreakable window

inside the room his anger
finger-knots   wrecking ball hard
swung at the end of flesh chains
bounce
off concrete walls

words   cracked
off the tip of a whip-tongue
draw blood from the air

spin back
down his throat
choke him into submission

      we stare at each other
      through an unbreakable window

outside the door
I check my pocket
for the big brass key

Mother Sometimes is Anger

this morning your words
splinter in the telephone line
we have talked about it before
how lucky you are to even
have a child at your age

how lucky I am not to
have a child at my age

this morning
you're caught in a frame of sunlight
cordless phone in one hand
the other one always ready to reach out
catch   wipe   swipe   dry   hold

you call me this morning
need to give me your anger
to say there are times when
you just don't want to be a mother
when you feel like a dark cloud hanging
in the eyes of your two-year-old

Alpha and Omega

for Ken Rivard

I

in the church I am startled
by light
where a friend's daughter is married

the sun paint-balls
the white walls
scores direct hits on the bride's white dress

catches words
in iridescent bubbles

II

the second time this year
I am in church

for a funeral
the mother of the friend whose daughter married
six months before

the light
sticks to the sallow walls
too heavy to lift

in front of the altar
my friend stands beside his mother's coffin
a knife of light
between them

Intersection

the windshield on my car
is the shield on a chariot
jockey for position
crowd the chariot beside me   wheels almost touching
driving to and from work

it is hard enough to block

       bumble bees that end
       their trip in a pollen-yellow splat

       diced bits of grey clouds and cold
       days that land with a whip-cracked smack

it isn't hard enough to protect me
from the intersection
of summer day and two cars

there wasn't any roar from a crowd
hanging in the hot air
only her small car
its windshield shattered into glass diamonds
her purse   chocolate bar wrapper   bag of dog food
and on the other side
of the centre line
a wool blanket covering her

Photo Album

three days out of five
he drives by the hospital
the wall reminds him of an open photo album

in the rows of rectangles
there should be faces smiling out at him
he searches each of the windows for recognition

cold sweat shudders down his back
he puts his foot on the accelerator
just a little harder than intended
breathes
only too glad
to realize this isn't the page
with his own picture on it   yet

Out a Window

for Lyn Thompson

he's in the hospital
wants to come home to
wait

the question opens
        wait for what?

the answer hangs
a drop of dew
at the end of a leaf outside the window
        to die

is this what dying is like?
daily trips to the hospital for one
but you both stare out a can't-open window
into sky

pleas to get the hell out of here
don't leave me here   not yet
take me with you
take me home

the room at the end
of the nurse's rounds
with the window in the door
nothing for her to do but
look in
before asking
is there anything I can get you?
what she doesn't say is
while you wait to die with him

yes damn it   there is
bring her   bring him
a clock with hands that don't move so fast
he is leaving
maybe tomorrow or the next day or
all she can do is take him home
hold his hand
until he slips through an open window
taking only his shadow with him

Colours of a Wake

for Lyle Weis

this morning there is
the sound of your mother's curtain pulled
from one side of a window to the other
blocking light threatening
to wake an old sleeper from her unfamiliar sleep

she closed her eyes finally
emptied them
while outside her window
lawn danced its dance
with a pheasant that made a surprise visit

you watched it for her
until a nurse closed
curtains the colour of pheasant feathers

opening your email
there is the sound of a curtain
shshshsh   shshsh

Down Sizing

after twenty years of being wrapped in newspaper
packed in a cardboard box marked
"mother's fine china tea cups"
tea party chatter is unwrapped

it is time to free up some storage room
we don't give tea parties
and there are no children to inherit

they are given to a friend
who holds each cup and saucer
fits them together as if she expected to feel
the cup fill

in her house
displayed behind unfamiliar glass doors
there is the illusion of
tea party chatter caught
between cup and saucer

her cups now
carefully washed
wait to be refilled

Building Security

the first thing he does
when he moves into the neighbourhood
is put security bars on all his windows

perhaps he sees the world
in grids of longitude and latitude
a cartographer
mapping his guarded coastline

or thinks with all those lines
his three daughters
would be unable to escape
the boundaries he set

or is afraid of home invasions
his daughters becoming Canadian girls
preferring cokes and fries to rice and stir-fried vegetables

the bars are not break-away
when we ask him how he will get out
in an emergency
one by one
he stops talking
to his neighbours

First Thunderstorm

the crash
lifts me off the bed
and I'm not sure in its aftermath
whether I cry out
or whether I just dream it

I watch the lightning scythe
the sky into bits and pieces
remember the first thunderstorm
you carried me to the window
we watched the light tear up the sky

what frightened me awake tonight
    crash of thunder
    fear that you aren't there now
    that I will have to explain
the flash of light
that obliterates
everything even memory

Peeping Tom

in the hot insanity
he walks up and down the summer afternoon
street by street

he takes his dog with him
not because dog's black coat will soak up the heat
but because he will soak up the cool stares of those who watch
from behind glass-glancing daylight curtains
and window blinds owner-pulled against the heat

they think they're safe
that he can't see in
will have to be content with the blank stares
houses give in return for his probing
besides they think they recognize the dog
and what harm can someone with a dog do

in the cool sanity
he slips back onto the same streets
house by house

he touches nothing
steals pieces of their back-lit lives

Window Blind

a boy slips up the back alley
on the last day of school before Christmas
hides his book bag and a note of apology
(for not being there for Christmases any more)
in a garbage can

a woman in the 2:00 a.m. parking lot
screams for help
like Kitty Genovese in 1964
her screams sliced out of her neck

a man walks to the bus every morning at 7:05
carrying his briefcase
comes back up the street at 5:30 every evening
his obituary catches everyone by surprise

while we are careful to match the decor
white   blue   green
venetian   pull down   sheer
we hang them in the windows
obscuring the view

Ninety Degrees to the Sun

up before the sun
their telephone call demands it

drive at ninety degrees to the morning
travel the day south to north
instead of east to west

this oversized sunrise washes over me
ignoring me behind the car windows
as it picks up colour off the already harvested field
on one side of the highway
and carries it to the farmer's house on the other side
smears the windows with gold veneer

I envy the farmer   his wife
from where I sit
their positions as daughter   son secure

I envy the sun
that washes across this highway

if I could
I would stop driving this road
at ninety degrees to the world

Shards of Sunday

summer still clings
in bits of crumpled yellow   orange   tired green
Fall whispers at the feet of trees
sun bounces smiles off the river valley

again we visit you
in the hospital
push open your door
you are standing
white hair and beard freshly combed
(you are just up from your usual nap)
you are ready

today we walk around the unit
your shuffle more of a step
with each step toward the next recognizable corner
of this well organized square world

you say how lovely
the flowers in the window box are
you miss the fact that they are artificial

we leave you
in a world of   doctors   nurses   artificial flowers
and meals eaten with table mates you would never
invite home for dinner
shards of your real world

Remembering for Two

on the telephone
I have to remember
what we are talking about
otherwise the words
loop back on themselves
open inward
on places we don't really mean to look

when I visit
you offer a drink
and I have to remember
I haven't taken a drink in years

in the apartment hallway
before going out for a drive
I have to ask if you have
your keys   wallet   watch
remind you to go to the bathroom

I have to remember
I am the child
because the words we use
want to turn in on themselves
and you are too willing to let them

The Windows

this morning on the commuter train downtown
I sit in the straight-backed seat
look past the guy who sits so easy
head resting on glass   eyes closed
across the aisle

there are a myriad of windows
     house windows splattered sunrise gold
     car windows tearing by trying to beat the train at its
own game
     sky-scraper windows putting on the day's make-up
     empty windows
     closed windows
     one way windows

everything blows by the glass on the other side of the aisle
trees wipe the irregular pieces of blue sky clear of cloud

at the end
I have not found what I wanted
the guy across the aisle
everything came to him while he waited
eyes still closed

No Way Out

inside the photograph album
the pictures are rows of windows

the pages are walls
he is pinned there by
faces framed
that look out
unable to open the windows
call out
in voices he struggles to remember

he wants to open the windows
from his side reach in
to arms that once pulled him in tight

wants the smell
fresh ironed cotton   wool suits
hair that has just been permed
the smell of warm skin

Tourist

tourists are easy to spot
camera   light meter
camera bag full of lenses
slung around necks

most things looked at
through the lens of the camera
everything framed by the black edges
of the viewfinder

> to give the best artistic impression
> get the best light

at home
stored on a shelf
in green plastic drawers
all the pictures
taken that year in a foreign country
colours fading
frame by frame

Pictures

on the dresser in the bedroom
between the penny jar and the cufflink box

on the file cabinet in the office
between the post-it notes and the inbox

from behind glass that bounces light
sometimes obliterates a face
they watch without comment
out of cheap frames of fake silver or gold
that hold them in

he wishes he had taken the time
to tell his mother how much he really loved her
to say to his father that their time suspended
in a hot-air balloon was the best time ever

there are times when
wrapping them in soft clean cloth
burying them in a dresser drawer
under sweaters somebody else bought
seems like a good idea

times when it would be easier to look at them
if he had used non-reflective glass in the frames

Shelf Life

on a storage room shelf
there is a nondescript box marked
"Dad's Date Books"

we open the box
lift his life out
year by year
spread fan-shape on the floor

pick through his days
year by year
looking for all the small spaces
where he fit us in

put them back chronologically
as if order really mattered now
close the top
flap by flap
shutters blocking any sight from the outside

This Abandoned Place

in the cove at the road's end
tide and winter storms have
ground their way back through sandstone layers
pushed the line between one year and the next
ahead of them

we have a picnic in grass almost too tall to see over
store-bought sandwiches and pop
about the same spot
as in the photograph album back home

explore a derelict house
Bay of Fundy coastal fog
the first lines of landing forces
obliterating the promises built here
the floor worn out by invaders' footsteps

in the flowerbed
        yellow Day Lilies
        Bachelor's Buttons
        Cosmos
continue the fight
not lost to the encroaching rabble

we walk backwards out of the yard
speak in reverent tones
don't raise a dust cloud as we drive away
down that road
don't disturb what's left behind

Kept on File

filing cabinets   four drawer   two drawer
military green   bland beige
they were the norm in our house
everything wound up in a file
everything

places of hidden mysteries
not the kind that made Christmas or a birthday
but more sombre ones
more fitting the rumble of steel on steel

ones we never spoke about
filed away under
L for love   H for hurt   N for need
as drawers ran out
slid back with a satisfying *ka-chunk*

the files you accumulated over years
of opening and closing those drawers
there was even a file with my name on it
you can't throw out now

the filing cabinets are gone
no room no need to keep secrets anymore

you asked me to dispose of them
you must have forgotten that I was there

Rear View Mirror

he didn't always worry
about getting caught unawares

used the bathroom mirror
stood on tiptoes
balanced on the sink edge
toothbrush tongue sticking out
pasted toothpaste giggles on the glass

stood in front of the mirror
twenty minutes or more
combing Score into his hair
to create just the right kiss-curl
a duck-tail any drake would be proud of

got a Safety razor for Christmas
weren't supposed to cut yourself
(so the package said)
stood in front of the mirror
searching out the three black hairs
nicked the tops of pimples
bled manhood passage into a sink
full of soft white soap turning pale pink

driving away from home the last time
watched house and parents
grow smaller
their images rattling on glass

now looking in the mirror
sometimes he gets caught
by something coming from behind
threatening to run him over

Reading about Life

in a bookshop on sixteenth avenue
we spend the first nice Spring Sunday
poets tell us about somebody else's life

hell there is life here too
the shelves in this store are stacked
floor to ceiling with it

we take it all very seriously
words in shouts   squeals   whispers
from the mouths of readers
backdropped by the street
that screams in blue and red flashing lights
going east
rumbles in eighteen forward gears
heading west

while quietly shelved second-hand words
and windows focus sunlight
from out there
on our word dust
hanging in the air in here

After Lunch in the Seniors' Home

each day they gather
on opposite sides of the craft table

on long sun-backed windows
there is a black outline of a hawk
stuck to the outside of the glass
its silhouette
warns off the sparrows

its shadow hunts the length of the room
makes no more sound than wind through feathers
along the ridges
where laughter lies
brushes the valleys of powder-soft shade
where tears often run river-swift
hovers over blue rivers
that glide quietly in worn channels

everybody watches

their hands flutter
over the edges of their work
take flight over landscapes of crocheting   knitting
picking up coloured yarns
weaving   tugging   tucking
patterns remembered by instinct

They

he can't remember talking to his grandparents
about getting old
they never said whether it was good or bad

he heard his parents
they said he was growing up too fast
never paid much attention

he never heard them
ask each other what might be ahead
but heard the old people in town
referred to as   they
            they can break a hip easy
            they can't cope much longer
            that's what happens when they get that age

he talks to his father
hears about
            eyes that won't see clearly
            water on the elbow
            no longer driving a car
he is told don't be in such a hurry
there is nothing golden about growing old
            not being able to remember

going home from visiting his parents
he tells himself all the way down the highway
how   they   are coping as well as can be expected

the first time
he drives all the way home without stopping
forgets the milk at the grocery store
he laughs about having too much on his mind

he hears himself
tell stories about old people
chuckles about calling them   they

fears a time when somebody he doesn't remember
will refer to him as they

Not Voyeurism

I can't be the only one
who includes it in his daily routine
turns on the TV at four
to watch Dr. Phil

who settles on the couch
in a sitting position
not prone
not this time
not broadcasting problems
to twenty million viewers

who waits until the commercial break
go to the bathroom
            (don't want to miss anything)
get a drink
            (glad not to answer "How's that working for ya?")

who watches somebody I don't know
cry their anger   hate
distrust for the people around them
can't imagine doing that in front of all those people

every day
turn the TV on
watch to see who won't find
that "ah ha" moment he is always talking about

After Thoughts on September 11

one day walking
in a long line to the front
you are passed by battalions
that have evacuated death
you ask what they've been through
one man walks behind another
one thing leads to another
        – Don Kerr, *In the City of Our Fathers*

standing safe and warm
in an early Fall day
watching shards
bodies
rain down
on unsuspecting pedestrians
from a perfectly clear blue sky

two buildings
designed to sway slightly in a high wind
that brooms the city clean
sway slightly in a morning without wind
stunned
not designed to accept airplanes
pushing faces out windows
they never looked out before

floors of windows folding themselves
like card towers
neatly straight down
almost as if they wanted to be sure
they didn't make more of a mess
than was necessary

long lines of people walking away
growing dust cloud of dreams
mushroom up
mask ghost-grey nightmares
firemen and policemen left to evacuate
the dead

Street Reflections

we pass them every day

each a homeless window into some other place   time
they lean precariously
against walls   bus benches

            where did they come from?
            why didn't they fit?

they are covered with their lives
we don't want to brush up against them

their frames cracked and peeling
the wind blows through their vacant spaces
their cries at night
dance against cold concrete
splinters of glass
glinting in the street light

we mutter about cleaning up the streets
pass them careful not to look too closely
not to look them in the eye
for fear we see our own reflection

Write from Your Roots

when I was a child I would open my mouth and suck and suck and suck and only nothing not air down my throat only the sound of nothing   whee hee whee hee   stuck in my throat and I was pushed in a wheelchair down down the hallway two floors up from here and nurse walking in shoes that squished softly so fast too fast not fast enough doors that opened inwards places   faces out of focus and I was pushed into one of the openings where there was a bed cold with sheets the colour of snow that matched my face and nurse slipped a mask over my face and I sucked and sucked and oxygen pushed open my throat and I could breathe and I looked out the window from a distance it was full of Spring-green light and my friends' parents driving cars and my friends playing outside and it protected me from the air outside while I breathed air from a tube and I waited for the day when I would grow up

when I could go home again

and when I was working here before I would push wheelchairs up and down these corridors and I wore shoes that squished softly pushed chairs so fast too fast not fast enough past openings along these corridors openings out of focus until I found the right opening this afternoon here I am two floors down the window behind me my background in focus and I am writing from my roots

Mathematics

I
mother was a statistician
she understood permutations and combinations
made those men of steel cry
told them no matter how big their chest measurements
how tough their bluff and bluster
she could guarantee their armour plate would be pierced
with real bullets during World War II

she juggled household columns of debit and credit
balancing them on either end of a pencil using tears for fulcrums
she knew the statistics on a woman having a healthy child
after the age of thirty-five fifty years ago
she knew the number of teens
who drank in the back seats of dark cars
the number of teens who tried to drive home after
without becoming one more statistic

her world wasn't all numbers
she didn't bother with the statistics on broken marriages
not believing hers would ever fall into one side of that ratio
until it did
she didn't know the numbers
people who drink themselves to death
after age sixty   didn't know the length of time it took
she didn't know the number of children who come home to find
their mother lying on the floor behind darkened windows

II
mother's world was a circle
she sailed around each of us
a moon
bonds far stronger than just gravity

she cut her circles with lines of radius
each segment separate
she knew exactly where each fit

after her divorce
her orbit began to disintegrate
the dimensions of her circle unclear
she saw her world from inside safety
the smooth surface of a rye bottle
she didn't remember the circumference of the bottle
gradually gets smaller
near the open end

Before the Window Falls

so which way do the shards of shattered glass fall?
does it really matter which side of the window
one is standing on when the glass breaks?
what if the window neither looks into something nor out of it
but is between what is now and what will be
between father and son

each walking away from the gaping hole
neither wanting to be caught holding it

each looking back wishing he might
somehow pick up the pieces
finish those things that father and son want to finish together
before the window falls and there is only one left

Christmas is Coming

I hung the ornaments
on the Norfolk Pine
in the dining room today

an 89-year-old man watched

at least I think he watched

he saved these decorations
from back home   they survived
the nicks and chips of Christmas
after Christmas   each unpacking
and packing again
he didn't even ask
what they were   never mind
where they came from

perhaps he knew what
I am just beginning to learn as
I pick each one out of the box
to hang   the branches bend more
from the added weight

The Day My Mother Died

the day before my mother died
I looked out the window of my office
into the blue cold sky

watched people walking into their new year
breath condensing
leaving small contrails across the parking lot

I watched through the windshield
the city roar and pass me
while I drove home leaving a trail
of exhaust lying on streets

I watched the ground drop away from me
through an airplane window my world fall into puzzle pieces
rectangles of dark earth side by side
with rectangles that had a gold tinge to them
pieces too big for me to handle and anyway
I couldn't reach them
watched it fall away from me
disappear into vapour of cloud

the day before my mother died
I looked out the window in the ICU
and all I could see was frost in the glass

the day my mother died was Epiphany

Something this Way Comes

the window is wide open and the blast of air it lets in is neither cool
nor refreshing it carries on its back smell   the smell of sweat off
long dead arguments real or imagined in the hollow dark of early
morning before the alarm rings   the smell of lilac scented Spring
mornings that will arrive too late to be enjoyed   the smell of
hospital cleaning fluids clean sheets puke and left over lunch
the window is wide open and there is nothing that can be done

Dancers of Night

they have always flirted with him

headlights from passing cars
slipping in between the spaces
in the venetian blinds frantic Tinkerbells
careening across bedroom walls

moon ball suspended
spins bouncing beams
deep across a shadow-raftered sky

lamppost sentries at attention
guarding the soft-shoe steps of unknown faces
over the straight and narrow concrete path

outside his window

Bubble

this morning we go grocery shopping
he looks straight ahead
and says I don't know who I am supposed to be

I tell him it is ok
I still know who you are
you are the man who bathed me as a baby
                         who was best man
at my wedding

it isn't ok damn it
he doesn't remember my bath
or the wedding
or the faces of people he is supposed to

we sit encased in the car
the glass holds the deadness in

getting out of the car
one of us leaves the bubble behind

Cut and Run

I look up at that window
stare at it from the sidewalk
it is our living room window
the light on the other side
means he is sitting in the La-Z-Boy
wearing two pairs of glasses
reading his book

on the sidewalk
I could turn right and walk north
or turn left and walk south

there are windows in both directions
but I don't have to look into
any of them if I don't want to

I could simply cut and run

instead I walk toward that window
each step on a two foot square of concrete
I find another piece of a smile
another word to go into the sentence
I will say as I open the door
I am glad you are here

Learning to See African

for Fern Langemann

your un-African eyes sweep back and forth
back and forth
across the inside of the windshield

there are so many recognizable tangled bits of field
it's the fragments of light and dark that stand out

the plants and animals are unfamiliar
except the ones learned from TV's Wild Kingdom
and then they were all in zebra black and white

this world comes in a jumble of frames
driving across country
and the colours are not black and white
but so bright they hurt

in the car your lap the easel for an open sketch book
you make black lines on white paper
grab bits of light to add colour later

you return home to tell stories in paintings
eyes sweeping side to side brushing colour

Surviving the Odds

she is out of hospital ten days
has survived the operation
hospital breakfast   lunch   supper
survived daily visits from friends
son   daughter   stepchild
well intentioned nurses
she has survived being called dear   sweetie   and Lady

survived her husband's absence
the dislocation of knives forks spoons
having somebody else in her kitchen

she has survived Christmas Eve and dinner
the multi-coloured blizzard of laughter wrapping
paper ribbons bows and tree lights

she has survived days marked
in calendar square lines
doors she can't leave through
walls that are closing in on her
just as the cancer she doesn't yet know about

today she survives by rejecting help offered
accusing us of talking behind her back

she survives by shouting at us
I still live here

Optics

there must be windows that laugh   allow
yellow sunlight to pool on the living room rug
the spot where the dog curls
eyes squeezed   muscles remembering
the dream that got away

somewhere there must be eyes
that allow light to crinkle
spill remembered laughter from their corners

notice how a window turns black?
not all at once
the darkness spreads from the middle
into the corners until
the last time you look
it has spread completely out to the edges

and when the glass is finally black
it is a mirror
throwing your face back into the room

Memory of Anger

mother was afraid she would leave
behind the memory of her anger

it lay just on the periphery
a thunderstorm on the horizon of her face
it would build there all day
air quilt thick
chairs   tables   everybody holding their collective breath
for that first crack of thunder to release them

mother was afraid of her own anger
so she used silence grey and sharp
or the way she put on her clip-on sunglasses

the day she moved out
she put on her sunglasses

click

clipping on anger

Caught Cleaning Windows

we've all seen her
the woman nobody knows
who cleans the windows
inside her house every week

she watches neighbours
mailman   dogs being walked
pass by her
through windows that hold her

she worries about streaks
the windows are real
stop her from stepping
into a world that will swallow her

Phobia

there are people who will not go
into the cool darkness of a cellar on a summer day
because of spiders or the dark
afraid they might be bitten

some who will not sit
in the shade of their gardens
when the relentless summer tyrant drives them from their homes
for fear bees or sun might sting them

there are people who will not emerge
from behind doors that used to open easily to their touch
secure in the knowledge that no one knows what
goes on behind closed doors

we drive past
the windows of the Home
refuse to look in for fear
some day one of those windows will be
the only view we have
the world driving by us
afraid to look in

Cancer Flowers

for years we've picked her favourite   carnations
presented them as a flag of truce

this time we step out of winter
pick tulips and daffodils
from buckets of Spring at Safeway

a peace offering placed beside the window
where she can see them
the flowers catch the late day sun
begin their dying too

From a Call Box

Stallworthy eschews metaphor in favour of the unadorned narrative. As with Tom Wayman, the "I" of Stallworthy's poems is often that curious but befuddled Everyman who smiles inwardly as if to acknowledge the fact that we're all bozos on this bus, but the sort of guy you trust and want to engage in conversation. Stallworthy is a good deal more economical with his phrasing and scene development than Wayman, and more inclined to keep you waiting for the punch line. His timing is as impeccable as the working class raconteur's; he knows when the coffee break ends, and how to keep you waiting until lunch.

~Richard Stevenson, *The Danforth Review*

For its historical range alone, *From a Call Box* is an interesting book, but when you add in the variety of human situations Stallworthy explores — a young man rehearsing a call for a date; lost conversations stored like peas in cans in a dead mother's pantry; a salesman making a "cold call" — you have a must read collection.

~Ronnie R Brown, *Canadian Bookseller*

From a Call Box is an extended metaphor in which the language of telecommunication is used to talk about the emotional limits of human communication... a valuable addition to the burgeoning literature about the effects, both positive and negative, of technology on our sense of community.

~Alexander Rettie, *Alberta Views*

Thomas Legg

Bob Stallworthy is a transplanted Maritimer who has lived in
Calgary for 25 years. He has been published in magazines and
anthologies across Canada, with two chapbooks of poetry and two
full length poetry books: *Under The Sky Speaking,* Snowapple Press,
1998, and *From a Call Box,* Frontenac House, 2001. He has
reviewed books for The Calgary Herald, CBC's Homestretch and
Eye-Opener, and was a poetry editor for Dandelion magazine. He has
given more than 150 readings and workshops complete with sound
effects and music. Bob, who was awarded the Calgary Freedom of
Expression Award in 2002, is a lifetime member of the Writers Guild
of Alberta and a full member of the League of Canadian Poets.